small craft

small
craft

JANET EDMONDS

DRAWINGS BY
LILY ROSA ALLEN

Sea Crow Press
amplifying voices

Small Craft
Published 2022 by Sea Crow Press
Paperback ISBN: 978-1-7358140-9-4
E-ISBN: 979-8-9850080-1-2
Library of Congress Control Number: 2022933098

Front Cover Images © Dianna Braginton-Smith
Cover Design by Popkitty Design
Interior Photography © Todd Viola (page 3); Janet Edmonds (pages 9, 25, 45)
Interior Art © Lily Rosa Allen
Interior Design by Mary Petiet

For information, address:
info@seacrowpress.com

In Memory of Nancy Lee Rose Edmonds,
My Mother, with Love

Contents

SMALL CRAFT

Advisories, in effect, are quiet calls
To mind nuances, signs of danger,
Notice wind speed, currents, rain clouds,
Use sense and so forth, head for port,
Harbor, haven, sturdy mooring –
Nautical warnings, gentle cries,
Slip away toward raised alarms of
Rain and spindrift spraying, breaking
Over edges, gunwales, hulls,
Drop.
Braced by shifting desolations,
Play of wind contends with waves.

COASTLINE
REFLECTIONS

SANDWICH

Out beyond the cranberry bogs,
There's a beacon,
And the smell of spring
Curling up from ages of peat

Flooded open by high tides,
Wafting marsh creeks flow to the harbor,
Mingle over stones and windrow,
Rolling in from Cape Cod Bay

BARNSTABLE

Past congestion of cottages,
Past Springhill Beach, East Sandwich Beach,
Great ridges of swept-up sand sweep
Down gaunt dunes to cove and legend:
An ancient woman of the sea
Lives in a cave past longshore drift,
Makes her home beside the harbor,
Each spring seeding woods and meadows,
Each fall reaping pods for magic,
Conjuror of tidal cycles,
Lunar days, and wheeling seasons,
Granny Squannit of the sea

CUMMAQUID

Marsh streams' riffles erode thick quiffs'
Astounding roots aggressively grasping
Composting hints of decades and centuries

Spoilage stippling tidal flats,
Breezes vexing supple tides,
Intransigent welter of finitude

DENNIS

Where landward spring and neap tides best
Tidal flats of bayside beaches,
Exigent winds around each year
Concur with ranges of the tides
And yield to telling periwinkles'
Trails unwinding on the sands:

Intricate journeys on offshore plains,
Swirls and loops and crosshatchings

CHATHAM

Sands of loss sweep in with Nauset
Curling up at Monomoy:
Recontouring by hurricanes,
That flout shores with impunity,
Leaves silhouettes of nature's wages

WELLFLEET

Venal tombolos hoarding sands,
Drift demurring on the berms,
Crescendos of breaking waves becoming
Softening echoes of slight swells
And wafting breezes in scrub pines

Beneath the gulls among the plovers,
Sylphing scent of bayberries
And industry of fiddler crabs

TRURO

Becoming rolling coastal dunes,
Head of the Meadow
And Ballston Beach,
Inchoate cusps and sandy ripples
Subsumed by longshore drift and rip tides
Rapt in timeless compromise:
Flooding, ebbing,
Swash and backwash,
Curved unanchored naked coastline
Shadowed by the austere scarp –

PROVINCETOWN

Across the dunes, the Province Lands:
Roiling crests crash the swash
And mulct the shore of every trace
Of time
And tracks
And tendered hand

Beyond Race Point, the breakwater:
A monument,
A shallow swale,
Opens on unending view

After the beach, the Woodend Light:
Echoes,
And a cache of glitter
Slipping up and down the waves

WATERCOLORS

Nicked across the crests of waves,
A sparkle flies off the blue
Background like stones skipped
In beach olympics:
Perfect–

And gone but caught
Again in your blue eyes
Landing on miracles:
A sea brick,
A starfish–

Camouflaged on autumn sands
With rose hip accents
And sturdy spartina
Spiking upwards:
Perfect–
Reflected in your eyes.

Tracing your way across tidal flats
Walking your cats in drizzles of snow,
Your gaze has reached from Salten Point
To Mussel Point and way beyond,
From Phillis Isle to Little Thatch,
From equinox to equinox.

Watching for weather across the harbor,
Reflecting silently on the dunes
Through fruitful, sere, and freezing seasons
Creating ways to see the world
With flickers, gulls, and cedar waxwings,
With finches, grackles, mourning doves,
With sparrows, robins, chickadees,
With ospreys, blue jays, cardinals,
Crows and starlings, sharp-shinned hawks
Eddying gently towards the sea.

From Beach Point to Green Point,
Slough Point to Blish Point,
Seeing what's before your eyes.

Suspended amid vagaries
Of lights beneath the surface blue
Sea glass in smooth opacities
Reneges on points that tear and wound
Fragments of broken summer days
Giving way to storm after storm
Before the seasons molt once more.

Green witness to translucent time
Remnant of some other shape
In lambent smithereens sent forth
Before the wrack and fractured ice
Balancing on soft waves riding
Under hoyden sea gulls seeking
Clams on edges of low tide.

And from the till of glacial dower
Advance retreating drift and sparkle
Lucent sea glass lens adjuring
Cleaned and recreated lines
Of wave, moraine, and boundary
In softly worn and sturdy focus.

You were walking up the road.

Tidal streams from wetland wainscots
Ease toward ebbing offshore ripples,
Shifting brinks of evanescence.

Early dawn relumes this harbor's
New spring canvas stretched for light strokes,
Backdrop neutrals, still-life shadows,
Monochrome of morning heron:
Oyster crown,
Jet epaulets,
Great slate wingspan,
Ashen down,
Turning inward between tide lines.

You, in turn, stalked mysteries.

WATER ALERT

This town's toxic waste dump opens
Twice a year only and requires a decal
On the windshield, residence, and fees paid,
Dues to not sneak fuels and paints and solvents,
Herbicides and pesticides and root growth
Hormone into drains and soils and sewers.
Consider the system of waterways,
Systems afflicted by influx of poisons,
Aquifer, rivers, feeders, and branches.
Consider mom's cancer and chemo today.

ABSENCE

On rising currents of warm air,
Seagulls' wingbeats whisper upward.
Cogent, steady, slow volutions
Ascending like a bird in space,
Cast to silent, smooth perfection,
Poised in softly poignant stillness.

Wood smoke cutting curves and figures,
Augurs of caprice and absence,
Piquant wisps around gray meadows'
Winter weeds and scattered fieldstones,
Touchstones of a way apart.
A cryptic, hallowed, quiet place.

BLUES

Wondrous welkin distal glidings
through cerulean blue serene
sapphire vistas, remote cobalt –
out of the blue, blue heron's beryl,
ultramarine firmament –

as cyan drifts toward dusking royal,
zaffer stars gleam astral patterns,
narrative delineations,
azure orbs in constellations'
tales of love and trust and patience –

mystic turquoise distant morning's
reticence as night retires
into the blue, blue soft light brush strokes–
heightened aquamarine ripples,
paint your certain flyway home

Winter Solstice

Exposure through development:
Light streaks of long nights' shooting stars
Darken to trails of dozens of starlings
Swooping through bruised Atlantic skies
Looking for berries, insects, and grubs.

This year's coda:
A short walk into the shortest day,
Pressed up flat against the wind-chill factor,
Heads bowed to white caps tipping by hundreds,
Splashing high tide over the boardwalk.

Footprints

What does it mean to watch whales dive?

Vast backs breaking through a surface,
White-marked jaws, fins, flukes, and plunge:
Footprints of a humpback whale–

Some huge smooth disturbance mirrored
Lucidly up here and hints,
Depths and reaches, unchecked, unplumbed.

After ripples cast forth gleanings,
You too rise to draw deep breaths,
Then thrust away beneath the questions.

CAPE COD NIGHT
LIGHTS

Navigating by Stars

This is a story with a univers-
al metaphor. Think of an odyssey,
journey, or voyage, a complex travers-
ing of miles and years. The speed of light
is an astounding one hundred eighty-
six thousand miles per second. That bright-
ness, flickering, or twinkling you see
right now traveled six trillion miles last year.

Navigators rely on that ancient light
as a kind of wisdom more true than clear
weather, as the northern hemisphere's bright-
est stars often shine through thick atmosphere's
pollution, haze, humidity, and re-
fraction laced with luminosity.

1. Regulus in Leo the Lion

The twenty-fifth brightest star, Regulus,
hugely dominating the summer sol-
stice looking blue and boasting luminos-
ity one hundred and forty times that
of our sun—impressive but not regal
and hardly the so-called "little king" at
the heart of Leo the lion, royal
guardian of heaven seen six thousand
years ago by ancient peoples who sat
back and guessed a ruling class should stake out land
in the heavens just so when they got
there they'd have a little something to command.

Regulus anchors its home constellation,
inverted question mark, fit punctuation.

2. DENEB IN CYGNUS THE SWAN

Sixteen hundred light years away and e-
qual to some sixteen thousand suns,
Deneb, the twentieth brightest star, re-
sides, near nebulae and the black hole X-1's
interstellar home in the Northern Cross
or Cygnus, the swan of the Milky Way,
eternally fixed in immortal loss
in interstellar dusty clouds. OK:
look at this metrically and run the num-
bers again: light travels three hundred thou-
sand kilometers per second and some-
where near nine or ten trillion per year. How
can anyone take that speed and distance
in in full, in stride, and maintain balance?

Gemini's moorings, two stars in a line,
appear in December and ride side by
side along the ecliptic, path of each sign's
zodiacal sea lane's directional lights.
The patterns of the constellations i-
ronically have no patterns despite flights
of imaginations, and the stars lie
far apart and unassociated
except as seen from Earth on clear nights
when Castor and Pollux seem separated
by inches, not light years caught in the whites
of vision's delusions, uncalibrated
by science's precise measurements, re-
search, experiments, and hypotheses.

4. ANTARES IN SCORPIO THE SCORPION

Conventions of narrative require plot
as well as characters, setting, and theme,
a rivalry resolved at some alott-
ed grim location, cold, remote, and gleam-
ing red five hundred light years away, ten
thousand times brighter than the sun and fift-
een times more massive. Vast Antares en-
gaged against not lookalike Mars but swift
self-immolation destined to precede
an overwhelming supernova set
to blow apart in an unsuperced-
ed huge explosion guaranteed to whet
appetites for special effects on grand-
er scales than theaters of wars command.

5. SPICA IN VIRGO THE MAIDEN

Another irony is that Virgo,
as associated with the goddess
of harvest, means "undefended," but o-
ver in Spring's east-southeast dusk she's one of
the largest constellations and, like Hes-
tia, commands serene awe but won't love
place or person long enough to address
questions about what the hearth means, what home
might be. She holds her ear of wheat above
her head, this maiden's Spica, blue-white chrome
star, sixteenth brightest and ready to shove
away from her port, too, only to roam.
Ten times more massive, two thousand times more
luminous than our sun's nuclear core.

Orange-reddish Aldebaran appears
in Taurus and the Hyades and seems
to sail behind the Pleides. Winter
night walks sixty-five million light years off
the mark can't resolve these myths into mean-
ingful stories, conquistadors of space
and time. Tales of sisters way beyond Mir's
meta-circumnavigations make reams
of meaningless text break down and inter-
pret the past, one cultural heritage scoff-
ing at another while the placid bull preens
for Europa – pretty, dull, and complac-
ent, and yet you do need a legend to
guide you on night walks through darkness.
You do.

Poetry will always throw you a line
and pull you toward safety through elements
as diverse as cosmic clouds, gas, and dust
as close as Altair in the Eagle just
seventeen light years off in the distance,
nine times as bright as the sun and defin-
ing the Summer triangle as Aqui-
la, yet another bird in space, falls free
through elements as diverse as line, rhyme,
dissonance, consonance, rhythm, and met-
rical patterns with regular stresses
or no stress depending on whether they mime
the meaning they tell of in form and met-
aphor – or none – as free verse digresses.

The foot of Orion is Rigel, an
incomprehensible nine hundred light
years away and sixty thousand times more
luminous than the sun. This is a huge,
hot, white star while dark red Betelgeuse deepl-
ly scars the hunter's shoulder and is e-
ven vaster than Rigel. One thousand
times wider than the sun, it will explode.
It will explode its cogent anguish in-
to incoherent brightness brighter than
a galaxy and brighter daily here
than the full moon would be if it were shin-
ing all day every day, but still this su-
pernova fades to dust and ashes, too.

Back to constellations, patterns, contexts:
legends and meanings are all about
safety. Polaris is always due north –
modest, steadying lodestar that reflects
the ancient wisdom navigators need,
yet profounder than a point of reference –
(back too to odysseys, journeys, voyages) –
leaning into inspiration to lead
seafarers through agitated danger,
high winds and waves in the middle of storms
so *almost* fierce enough to crack apart
hulls and decks completely, but don't. Stranger
things have happened, say recovery crews. You
have to be prepared for wrecks.
You do.

WALKING

Discontinuities and dislocations,
Images and disconnections –

In the middle of my life I suppose
I might sigh and look and know what these mean,
Yet so far only grim memento mori
Visit from past shadowed embarkations,
Adumbrations, vague distractions,
Leaves disturbed on unmarked trails.

TAPPING SEASON

There's science to just about everything:
Sap sugar content depends on the trees,
Sap sugar flow depends on the weather,
Confluence of seasons, winter with spring.

Drill with a sharp seven-sixteenths inch bit.
Tap before maples mature and break bud.
Tap as Arcturus ascends the horizon.
Light-colored sapwood, riven, spills over.

Spring

Sleet-slashed salt squall slapped back spring so far each
Dogwood, cherry, lilac blossom, petal
Burst and broke and blew down so intensely
Thick and fixed and far –
New galaxies.

STONE WALLS

Ice ages ago, miles-high glaciers reft
hills and fields of soil and left
rocks of every shape and size strewn
poised to bend and break the ploughs that broke
the beasts that pulled them and the earth
as it gave way to crops at last
and later roads and towns and suburbs,
demarcated plots and subplots,
old walls, cumbrous, tumbling, broken.

Repairs require patient precision,
hammers, chisels, muscles, vision:
in fallow fields, lost wooded farm lots,
locate stones for reconstruction,
separate by form and function
(end stones, base stones, cross stones, shim stones),
attendants of stability
and steady, sturdy laws of walls,
freestanding ramparts, worthy bastions,
braced by balance, leaning inward.

Cape Cod Minutes

1. Asters

Hues and hoopla across the spectrum
Lining riverbeds, roadsides, meadows,
Radiant petals' songs through autumn,
Perennial pictograms, shooting stars

2. Spring Tides

Disporting with each new and full moon,
Tuned to waxing lunar cycles,
High tides leap past boundaries,
Lows sweep back to open seas

3. Slack Water

Sum of currents' tidal cycles,
After ebb tides, before flood tides,
After flood tides, before ebb tides,
Sacred stillness, silent waters

4. Dunes

Past splash and spray zone, beach grass grasping,
Heather, pitch pine stands stand clasping
Sands to windward steep exposures,
Roots to sloping leeward shoulders

5. Surf Zone

Fomenting winds force sculling offshore waves
To crest and burst toward glowing lodestars
Shining every way and which way
Pointing to particulars

6. Flood Current

Advancing yearning, yawing day and night,
Glimmering tricky luminescence mingles
Woven ripples, hastened rhythms
Here and there against an inlet's limits

7. Sand

Each page of wind and ice grinds out
Sharp or rounded tales from history,
Eroded fossils, rocks, and minerals,
Grains drift shifting into time

8. Spindrift

Chronicles of indistinctions,
Sprayed conceits on dim horizons,
Pointillist depictions merging
Places, shapes with memories

Cattails

9. Barnacles

Larval adventurers, neonates seeking,
Surfing for homes along rocky shorelines,
Vestments cemented on coastal moorings,
Six-sided downslopes, galactic addresses

10. Marsh Hawk

Long-tailed, long-winged swoop from woodlands
Gliding low through meadows scanning,
Raptor glints for reptiles, mammals —
Rash, swift, silent devastation

11. Humpbacks

Feeding ground's rhapsodic frolic,
Water dance of cows' and calves'
Flippings, dippings, rotund tumblings,
Fluke propulsions, arching breachings

12. Cattails

In rushes among phragmites, reeds
Rustle rushing snares above long runners,
Narrow-leaved with thick tops leaning,
Bowing brown to brackish acres

13. Red Squirrel

Disputing boundaries, marking parcels,
Russet tinhorn's chatter trumpets
Pugilistic piffle, warnings,
Screechy ceaseless preachings from on high

14. Meadow

Shadowy voles from shrubbery covers,
Intermittent speedy scampers,
Over stubble, under new growth,
Tinted ramparts, tilted trailings

15. Swells

Chords of orbits, winds, and tides,
Out of southeast gusty galings,
Undulating aqua pulsars,
Gifts of rolling gravity

16. Great Horned Owl

Clean snatch captured, tolls of talons,
Half-light's heavy thick-set shadows,
Rhythmic half hoots, whole hoots, callings,
Hooded mantled eyes observing all

17. Sandbars I

Along shores, longshore's currents carving,
Arching paths for sand, stone, rubble,
Streaming beach drift tumbling, reaching,
Sifting, settling, resting under seas

18. Big Dipper

Ungentle long-lost nascencies,
Expanding spiral galaxies,
Touching near event horizons,
Clustered light years, huddles of stars

19. Harbor

Soft scintillated edges, bittersweet,
Exquisite brilliance, trills of flickers;
Moorings pull in deepened light
And squalls of startled terns ascending

20. Peepers

Fertile young dusk, bogs and ponds,
Familiars, spring-time pinkwinks peep,
Tiny tree frogs scaling tree trunks
Chirping silly stories after all

21. Quahogs

Burrowed, buried, fine-lined, hard-shelled
Homes in intertidal substrates,
Beady boon for natives trading
Wampum treasures, cherrystone lore

22. Wrack

Strewn by storm and strong surf, flotsam,
Knotted, tangled kelp and rockweed
Rolling down uncoiling crests
Toward clemencies of ebbing seas

23. Inlets

Over spear points, stoneware, chilled hearths,
Trails of Wampanoag walking,
Shoaling between islands, streaming,
Shaping shores' new boundaries

24. Eastern Cottontails

Dawn's briary havens, warrens issue
Crinkly, wrinkling noses, muscles,
Testing, scenting danger's presence,
Dappled, wary, sudden prey

Quahogs

25. Perigean Tides

New moon's, full moon's gravitation,
Luminary touchings, torchings,
Freshets flooding over tidelands'
Tidings of far-reaching rangings

26. Fireflies

In sparkling mating dances high
And low across meadows and branches
Limning a lightsome sketch of amaze
Elucidating legends for long lives

27. Rainbow

Ascension of raindrops refracting reflections
Of ages and places traversing the harbor,
Spectral covenants against the dark—
Where there is nothing, there is what's there

28. Osprey

Mysterious gliding, tenacious flight,
Steep plunge, hunter's deathly gesture,
Solo circlings, surveys, searchings,
Pinioned armor, feathered vesture

29. Sirius

Shimmering blue-bright, double-scorched,
Leaning softly on winter's horizon,
Climbing spring and riding summer,
Sleights of hand, delightful dog star

30. Starfish

Treasures of foreshore firmaments,
Champions of scouring rip tides,
Baleful undertowing powers,
Enthroned and sand-strewn archangels

31. Sea Lavender

Sparkling unfettered purple-spangled,
Tiny tangled flares and mirrors
Constellating marsh-lined shores,
Scintillating season's flowers

32. Polaris

Lexical light tricks, flashes, encodings,
Old salts reading old directions,
Orb unmoved for exploration,
Circumnavigators' Pole Star

33. Great Blue Heron

Against a weight of silent dawns and dusks,
Recurrences of spearings, joustings,
Momentary musings on delights,
Tasty schools of minnows flicker by

34. Fog

Shadows' obfuscations scrimmage,
Fumble, groping for discernment,
Outlines, definitions, sure of
Gentle guidelines against darkness

35. Moon

Casting halos, luminescence,
Sheer sheen's waxing bold reflections,
Silent waning, gentle dances,
Origins of mysteries

36. Apogean Tides

Celestial trickery re-receding,
Range decreasing empties tideways,
Mute dejection, full abandon,
Absent incidental losses

37. Eastern Coyotes

Den is in thick hillside brambles
Nettlesome against intrusions,
Choral howls, numbers' collusions,
Suddenly a coup de grace

38. Tombolo

Sites of old tryworks, ports for old whalers,
Boilers of blubber, meandering travelers
Over brief coursings of centuries' waves,
Sand bridges, oil, connect present with past

39. Windrow

Mowed by cold and short days, marsh hay,
Tumbled rows along high tide lines,
Deep, dense heaps of cord and beach grass
Settle down to deeper time

40. Razor Clams

Low flats' quick, deep burrowers
Splayed alongside rippling tipples,
Musterers of siphons powers
Flash in bubbles, disappear

Bullfrogs

B

41. Bullfrogs

Harbingers of equal days and nights,
Huddled in fresh swamps and pools,
Groggy grownup tadpoles sporting spring legs
Bellyflops, thick burps, croaks, and mating calls

42. Bay

Anchorage for fluent whitecaps,
Port of flux, of tidemarks, ranges,
Haven, harbor, inlet, bight—
Windjammer, wearied, wandering home

43. Orion

Stately dance gives way to leaps—
Hunter vaults into the sky,
Expanding fields of ancient dust,
Great scabbard bearing nebulae

44. Sandbars II

And under shallow ripplings, ridges rising,
Curving landward, reaching inward,
Leeward gusts and shore drift thrusting
Bay mouth bars toward harbors' closure

45. Tern

Coal-capped, plunging, almost omnivore,
Streaming, hovering, dropping deep and fast,
Predator of ocean, bay, and beach:
Aerial grace and joie de vivre

46. Breakers

Strummy rapid riffs of jet spray breaking
Over coving landward troughs toward slaking
Misted oblique shores with flotsam,
Presents of stormy visitations

47. New Field

Thick through loamy conjurations,
Clover over wintered milkweed,
Greenery from fallow furrows,
Sustenance of ancient tilling

48. Gray Squirrel

Acrobatic leaps, surprising sweeps,
Pithy sweet swift arcs, light scuffles,
Jaunty tiffs for corncobs, acorns—
Raucous play for grace at harvest

49. Fieldstones

Seasonal thawing, granite upheavals,
Igneous intrusive, slow-cooled
Feldspar, garnet, metamorphic,
Deep beneath this mantle, shifting

50. Pilot Whales

Synchronous cavalcading curvets,
Rollicking dorsals clipping, skipping,
Ebony-sleek, finned capering pods,
Balletic vaults approaching inlets

51. Sandpipers

Aplomb and dazzled clash toward magic
Long-billed, leggy skippers of these shores,
Darting inward, outward lines and curves—
Trajectories, topographies of time

52. Spume

Tide-rip's tropes, timpanic rollers,
Surf of bursting repercussions',
Cymbals crashing, thrashing meaning,
Froth and foam along the shore

Fiddler Crabs

53. Fiddler Crabs

Embattled clawed cartographers
Charting mud flat properties marsh expanses, darting
Darting ways away from burrows,
Casting over open seas

54. Beach Grass

Blades pirouette and loosely bow,
Tracing smiles of slight regret –
Tenacious roots hold forth this world
Of sand, of hearties' fiddlestick homes

55. Ebb Current

Mingling mud flats' sounds and smells,
Mixes, blends of outward trickles,
Pungent weavings, vital signs,
Warp and woof of tidal gleanings

56. Spray Zone

Scumbling spray transects horizons,
Scudding white caps crashing headlong,
Salt-soaked, rock-strewn, bouldered coastline,
Spindrift bursts in all directions

57. Swales

Down flanking dunes, protected hollows,
Mossy, spurgy, grassy shallows
Tucked among round dimpled shadows,
Wantonly, concavities

58. Tidal Cycles

Out of stillness, quiet waters,
Celebrants of changes' rhythms,
Steady downbeats pressing tide lines,
Sums of currents' ebbings, floodings

59. Neap Tides

Cavorting with midway lunar phases
Molting fortes, high and lows,
Slight attunements, tender reaches,
Softly touching, gravity

60. Earth Stars

Repeated tans, deep taupes, soft duns:
Unlikely puffballs line beach hollows,
Ripened, rounded novas bursting,
Earth stars scatter spores to wind

Earth Stars

LOCAL RADAR

Rain, heavy at times, saturates and pools
Over surfaces so sealed off, packed down,
So scarred with deadened aspect
Nothing grows here anymore.

We've raked this space so many times before,
Built up, reseeded, tended, marked off, drained,
We've cut back limbs to clear ways for a warmth
To light and rest and spread its roots beyond
The reach of any tempest's, any downpour's
Wrenching grasp and still won't give up, give in:
We turn the soil and make this place for prayer.

About the Author

Janet Edmonds spent childhood summers in the lush Adirondacks where she explored and played, making forts and fairy houses with her sisters, in woods filled with freshwater ponds and brooks. After teaching delightful high school students in Connecticut, she inched a bit closer to the ocean by digging into nearly thirty years of editorial work in Boston near the Seaport District. During that time on a quick getaway to Cape Cod, she recognized herself as a sand and saltwater person. Her soles and soul sizzled with happiness during her first wintry walk on Sandy Neck followed by an icy hike on Race Point Beach in Provincetown. A year later she moved to Barnstable and started to write poetry about her experiences and observations here. *Small Craft* is her first book.

By the grace of corporate downsizing, she gave up a twenty-five year daily bus commute and now spends her days near a salt marsh and harbor. She grows scores of daylilies and hostas, carves and shapes wood burls, writes, and feels endlessly thankful for a never-expected abundance of loving, fun, and gracious friends. She is grateful to all of them all of the time.

About the Artist

Lily Rosa Allen is a visual artist and design student based in Brooklyn, NY. Born and raised on Cape Cod, she enjoys drawing inspiration from local ceramicists and environments.

Her current works can be found online
at www.lilyrosaallen.com

ABOUT THE PRESS

Sea Crow Press is committed to amplifying voices that might otherwise go unheard with a focus on positive change and great storytelling. Founded in 2020, the growing press is home to an eclectic collection of creative nonfiction, fiction, and poetry. At Sea Crow Press we believe the small press plays an essential part in contemporary arts by amplifying its voices. Sea Crow Press is committed to building an accessible community of writers and dedicated to telling stories that matter.

Sea Crow Press is named for a flock of five talkative crows you can find anywhere on the beach between Scudder Lane and Bone Hill Road in Barnstable Village on Cape Cod.

According to Norse legend, one-eyed Odin sent two crows out into the world so they could return and tell him its stories. If you sit and listen to the sea crows in Barnstable as they fly and roost and chatter, it's an easy legend to believe.